MW00513772

The Ultimate Air Fryer Cookbook

How To Cook Your Easy And Healthy Favourite Fried Meals

Joana Smith

© Copyright 2021 - All rights reserved.

The content contained within this book may not be reproduced, duplicated or transmitted without direct written permission from the author or the publisher.

Under no circumstances will any blame or legal responsibility be held against the publisher, or author, for any damages, reparation, or monetary loss due to the information contained within this book. Either directly or indirectly.

Legal Notice:

This book is copyright protected. This book is only for personal use. You cannot amend, distribute, sell, use, quote or paraphrase any part, or the content within this book, without the consent of the author or publisher.

Disclaimer Notice:

Please note the information contained within this document is for educational and entertainment purposes only. All effort has been executed to present accurate, up to date, and reliable, complete information. No warranties of any kind are declared or implied. Readers acknowledge that the author is not engaging in the rendering of legal, financial, medical or professional advice. The content within this book has been derived from various sources. Please consult a licensed professional before attempting any techniques outlined in this book.

By reading this document, the reader agrees that under no circumstances is the author responsible for any losses, direct or indirect, which are incurred as a result of the use of information contained within this document, including, but not limited to, errors, omissions, or inaccuracies.

Table Of Contents

DESCRIPTION

The history of Air fryers dates back to a few years ago; exactly during the third quarter of the year 2010 and it was a completely revolutionary invention that was invented by Philips Electronics Company. Philips introduced the Air Fryer to the world and changed the conception of the culinary world all at once.

The Air Fryer is used as a substitute for your oven, stovetop, and deep fryer. It comes with various handy parts and other tools that you can buy to use your Air Fryer for different cooking styles, which include the following:

• Grilling. It provides the same heat to grill food ingredients without the need to flip them continuously. The hot air goes around the fryer, giving heating on all sides. The recipes include directions of how many times you ought to shake the pan during the cooking process.

To make the process of grilling faster, you can use a grill pan or a grill layer. They will soak the excess fat from the meat that you are cooking to give you delicious and healthy meals.

- Baking. The Air Fryer usually comes with a baking pan (or you can buy or use your ownto make treats that are typically done using an oven. You can bake goodies, such as cakes, bread, cupcakes, muffins, and brownies in your Air Fryer.
- Roasting. It roasts food ingredients, which include vegetables and meat, faster than when you do it in the oven.
- Frying is its primary purpose – to cook fried foods with little or no oil.

You can cook most food items in an Air Fryer. There are some foods that you should refrain from cooking in the fryer because they will taste better when cooked in the traditional ways — they include fried foods with batter and steamed veggies, such as beans and carrots.

Despite this, you will never run out of ingredients to cook using your Air Fryer – from veggies to seafood, chicken, egg, turkey, and a lot more. The most common component that is prepared using this appliance is potatoes.

The Air Fryer also comes with a separator, and this allows you to cook multiple dishes at the same time. You need to choose recipes that can be prepared at the same temperature setting.

This book covers the following topics:

- Breakfast
- Mains
- Sides
- Seafood
- Poultry

INTRODUCTION

There are many kinds of foods that you can cook using an air fryer, but there are also certain types that are not suited for it. Avoid cooking ingredients, which can be steamed, like beans and carrots. You also cannot fry foods covered in heavy batter in this appliance.

Aside from the above mentioned, you can cook most kinds of ingredients using an air fryer. You can use it to cook foods covered in light flour or breadcrumbs. You can cook a variety of vegetables in the appliance, such as cauliflower, asparagus, zucchini, kale, peppers, and corn on the cob. You can also use it to cook frozen foods and home prepared meals by following a different set of instructions for these purposes.

An air fryer also comes with another useful feature - the separator. It allows you to cook multiple dishes at a time. Use the separator to divide ingredients in the pan or basket. You have to make sure that all ingredients have the same temperature setting so that everything will cook evenly at the same time.

The Benefits of Air fryer

It is important to note that air fried foods are still fried. Unless you've decided to eliminate the use of oils in cooking, you must still be cautious about the food you eat. Despite that, it clearly presents a better and healthier option than deep-frying. It helps you avoid unnecessary fats and oils, which makes it an ideal companion when you intend to lose weight. It offers a lot more benefits, which include the following:

- It is convenient and easy to use, plus, it's easy to clean.
- It doesn't give off unwanted smells when cooking.
- You can use it to prepare a variety of meals.

CHAPTER 1

BREAKFAST

1. Pepper Stuffed Spinach Parmesan Baked Eggs

Preparation time: 5 minutes • Cooking time: 14 minutes • Servings: 2

INGREDIENTS

- 4 eggs

- 2 Tbsp heavy cream

- 2 Tbsp frozen, chopped spinach, thawed

- 2 Tbsp grated parmesan cheese

- ½ tsp salt

- 1/8 tsp ground black pepper

- 1 large red pepper, cut in half vertically, seeds removed

DIRECTIONS:

1. Preheat your air fryer to 330 degrees F.

2. Place red pepper halves in the air fryer basket and cook for 5 minutes.

3. In a small bowl, whisk together all the ingredients

4. Pour the eggs into the partially cooked peppers and bake for 7 minutes.

5. Enjoy straight out of the baking cup!

NUTRITION: Calories 189, Total Fat 11g, Saturated Fat 4g, Total Carbs 5g, Net Carbs 3g, Protein 14g, Sugar 2g, Fiber 2g, Sodium 134mg, Potassium 148g

2. Pepper Stuffed Spinach and Feta Eggs

Preparation time: 5 minutes • Cooking time: 14 minutes • Servings: 2

INGREDIENTS

- 4 eggs 2 Tbsp heavy cream

- 2 Tbsp frozen, chopped spinach, thawed

- ¼ cup feta crumbles

- ½ tsp salt 1/8 tsp ground black pepper

- 1 large red pepper, cut in half vertically, seeds removed

DIRECTIONS:

1. Preheat your air fryer to 330 degrees F.

2. Place red pepper halves in the air fryer basket and cook for 5 minutes.In a small bowl, whisk together all the ingredientsPour the eggs into the partially cooked peppers and bake for 7 minutes.

3. Enjoy straight out of the baking cup!

NUTRITION: Calories 192, Total Fat 11g, Saturated Fat 6g, Total Carbs 5g, Net Carbs 3g, Protein 14g, Sugar 2g, Fiber 2g, Sodium 156mg, Potassium 148g

3. Basil-Spinach Quiche

Preparation time: 10 minutes • Cooking time: 10 minutes •

Servings: 4

INGREDIENTS

- ½ cup spinach

- 1 oz fresh basil, chopped

- 1 oz walnuts

- 3 eggs

- ¾ cup almond milk

- ½ teaspoon salt

- 1 tablespoon almond flour

DIRECTIONS

1. Chop the spinach and combine it together with the chopped basil.

2. Crush the walnuts and add them to the green mixture too.

3. After this, add the salt and almond flour.

4. Stir the mixture and place it in the air fryer basket.

5. Then beat the eggs in the separate bowl and whisk well.

6. Add almond milk and stir carefully.

7. Pour the egg mixture over the greens and cook it for 10 minutes at 375 F.

8. When the quiche is cooked – let it chill well and serve!

NUTRITION: Calories 237, Fat 21.8, Fiber 2.4, Carbs 5.3, Protein 8.7

4. Nutmeg Mushroom Fritters

Preparation Time: 2hrs. 11 Minutes • Servings: 8

INGREDIENTS

- Mushrooms, chopped -4 ounces

- Red onion, chopped-1

- Salt and black pepper -to taste

- Nutmeg, a ground-¼ tbsp.

- Olive oil- 2 tbsp

- Panko breadcrumbs -1 tbsp.

- Milk -10 ounces

DIRECTIONS

1. Add 1 tbsp oil to a suitable pan and place it over medium-high heat.

2. Stir in mushrooms and onions, sauté for 3 minutes.

3. Add nutmeg, pepper, salt, and milk.

4. Take it off the heat and keep it aside for 2 hours.

5. Mix remaining oil with breadcrumbs in a separate plate.

6. Take a tbsp of the mushroom mixture and roll it.

7. Coat this ball with breadcrumbs mixture then flatten it.

8. Place it in the Air fryer basket.

9. Repeat the same steps and place the fritters in the basket.

10. Seal it and cook for 8 minutes at 400 o F on Air fryer mode.

11. Serve warm.

NUTRITION: Calories: 202, Fat: 8g, Fiber: 1g, Carbs: 11g, Protein: 6g

5. Tofu & Bell Peppers Medley

Preparation Time: 15 Minutes • Servings: 8

INGREDIENTS

- Yellow bell pepper, cut into strips-1

- Orange bell pepper, cut into strips -1

- Green bell pepper, cut into strips -1

- Salt and black pepper -to taste

- Firm tofu, crumbled-3 ounces

- Green onion, chopped-1

- Parsley, chopped-2 tbsp.

DIRECTIONS

1. Take a pan, suitable to fit your Air fryer.

2. Add bell pepper strips along with remaining things.Toss well then place the pan in the Air fryer basket.Seal it and cook for 10 minutes at 400 o F on Air fryer mode.Serve warm.

NUTRITION: Calories: 135, Fat: 2g, Fiber: 2g, Carbs: 8g, Protein: 3g

6. Stuffed Feta Cheese Peppers

Preparation Time: 13 Minutes • Servings: 8

INGREDIENTS

- Small bell peppers, tops cut off and seeds removed-8

- Avocado oil -1 tbsp.

- Salt and black pepper -to taste

- Feta cheese, cubed-3½ ounces

DIRECTIONS

1. Toss cheese with oil, salt, and pepper in a bowl.

2. Stuff the peppers with cheese mixture then place these peppers in the Air fryer basket.

3. Seal the fryer and cook for 8 minutes at 400 o F on Air fryer mode.

4. Serve warm.

NUTRITION: Calories: 210, Fat: 2g, Fiber: 1g, Carbs: 6g, Protein: 5g

CHAPTER 2

MAINS

7. Air Fried Dragon Shrimp

Cooking Time: 15 minutes Servings: 2

INGREDIENTS

- ½ lb. shrimp

- ¼ cup almond flour

- Pinch of ginger

- 1cup chopped green onions

- 2tablespoons olive oil

- 2eggs, beaten

- ½ cup soy sauce

DIRECTIONS

1. Boil the shrimps for 5-minutes. Prepare a paste made of ginger and onion. Now, beat the eggs, add the ginger

paste, soya sauce and almond flour and combine well.

Add the shrimps to the mixture then place them in a

baking dish and spray with   oil.   Cook   shrimps

at 390°Fahrenheit for 10-minutes.

NUTRITION: Calories: 278, Total Fat: 8.6g,

Carbs: 6.2g, Protein: 28.6g

8. Lasagna Zucchini Cups

Cooking Time: 25 minutes • Servings: 6

INGREDIENTS

- Chopped parsley, for garnish

- ¼ cup parmesan, freshly grated

- ½ cup mozzarella, shredded

- ½ cup ricotta

- 1-14.5-ounce can of crushed tomatoes

- Black pepper and salt to taste

- ½ teaspoon oregano, dried

- ½ lb. ground beef

- 2garlic cloves, minced

- ½ onion, chopped

- 1tablespoon olive oil

- 3zucchinis

DIRECTIONS

1. n a large pan over medium heat, add the oil. Add onion and garlic and cook for 5- minutes. Add in

the ground beef and cook for 10-minutes stirring often. Season with oregano, salt, pepper, cook until meat is no longer pink. Add crushed tomatoes and simmer mixture for 5-minutes. Stir in the ricotta and remove from heat. Cut zucchini in half crosswise in two. Using a spoon scoop out zucchini flesh to create wells. Fill wells with meat mixture. Top with mozzarella and parmesan cheese. Place directly in air fryer and cook at 350°Fahrenheit for 15-minutes. Garnish with parsley and parmesan.

9. Spinach Artichoke Stuffed Peppers

Cooking Time: 15 minutes • Servings: 4

INGREDIENTS

- 4assorted bell peppers,

- halved and seeded

- Salt and black pepper to taste

- Olive oil for drizzling

- 2cups shredded rotisserie chicken

- Fresh parsley, chopped for garnish

- 2cloves garlic, minced

- ¼ cup mayonnaise

- ¼ cup sour cream

- ½ cup mozzarella, shredded, divided

- 6-ounces cream cheese, softened

- 1(10-ouncepackage   frozen   spinach,   thawed, well-drained, and chopped

- 1(14-ouncecan artichoke hearts, drained and chopped

DIRECTIONS

1. On a large, rimmed baking sheet, place bell peppers cut side-up and drizzle with olive oil, then season with salt and pepper. In a large bowl, combine chicken, artichoke hearts, spinach, cream cheese, ½ cup mozzarella, parmesan, sour cream, mayo and garlic. Season with more salt and pepper and mix until well blended. Divide the chicken mixture between pepper halves, top with remaining mozzarella, and bake in air fryer at 400°Fahrenheit for 15- minutes. Garnish with parsley and serve.

NUTRITION: Calories: 284, Total Fat: 13.4g, Carbs: 9.2g, Protein: 34.3g

10. Cauliflower Stew with Tomatoes and Green Chilies

Preparation time: 10 minutes • Cooking time: 15 minutes • Servings: 4

INGREDIENTS

- 30ounces canned cannellini beans, drained
- 4cups cauliflower florets
- 1yellow onion, chopped
- 28ounces canned tomatoes and juice
- 4ounces canned roasted green chilies, chopped
- ½ cup hot sauce
- 1tablespoon stevia
- 2teaspoons cumin, ground
- 1tablespoon chili powder
- A pinch of salt and cayenne pepper

DIRECTIONS

1. In your air fryer's pan, mix cannellini beans with cauliflower, onion, tomatoes and juice, roasted green

chilies, hot sauce, stevia, cumin, chili powder, salt and cayenne pepper, stir, cover and cook at 360 degrees F for 15 minutes.

2. Divide into bowls and serve hot.

3. Enjoy!

NUTRITION: Calories 314, Fat 6, Fiber 6, Carbs 29, Protein 5

11. Simple Quinoa Stew

Preparation time: 10 minutes Cooking time: 15 minutes Servings: 6

INGREDIENTS

- ½ cup quinoa
- 30ounces canned black beans, drained
- 28ounces canned tomatoes, chopped
- 1green bell pepper, chopped
- 1yellow onion, chopped
- 2sweet potatoes, cubed
- 1tablespoon chili powder
- 2tablespoons cocoa powder
- 2teaspoons cumin, ground
- Salt and black pepper to the taste
- ¼ teaspoon smoked paprika

DIRECTIONS

1. In your air fryer, mix quinoa, black beans, tomatoes, bell pepper, onion, sweet potatoes, chili powder,

cocoa, cumin, paprika, salt and pepper, stir, cover and

cook on High for 6 hours.

2. Divide into bowls and serve hot.

3. Enjoy!

NUTRITION: Calories 342, Fat 6, Fiber 7, Carbs 18, Protein 4

12.Green Beans with Carrot

Preparation time: 10 minutes Cooking time: 12 minutes Servings:

4

INGREDIENTS

- 1pound green beans

- 1yellow onion, chopped

- 4carrots, chopped

- 4garlic cloves, minced

- 1tablespoon thyme, chopped

- 3tablespoons tomato paste

- Salt and black pepper to the taste

DIRECTIONS

1. In your air fryer's pan, mix green beans with onion, carrots, garlic, tomato paste,, salt and pepper, stir, cover and cook at 365 degrees F for 12 minutes.

2. Add thyme, stir, divide between plates and serve.

3. Enjoy!

NUTRITION: Calories 231, Fat 4, Fiber 6, Carbs 7, Protein 5

13.Crunchy Chicken Fingers

Preparation time: 15 minutes • Cooking time: 12 minutes • Servings:

4

INGREDIENTS

- 12oz chicken fillet

- ½ cup coconut flakes

- 2eggs

- ¼ cup almond milk

- 1tablespoon almond flour

- ½ teaspoon chili flakes

- ½ teaspoon salt

- ½ teaspoon ground black pepper

- tablespoon olive oil

DIRECTIONS

1. Cut the chicken fillet in the shape of the fingers.

2. Then take the bowl and beat the eggs in it.

3. Whisk the eggs and add almond milk and almond

   flour.

4. Then add the chili flakes and salt.

5. Sprinkle the mixture with the ground black pepper and whisk it well until homogenous.

6. Dip the chicken fingers in the egg batter and after this, coat them in the coconut flakes.

7. Pour the olive oil into the air fryer basket and place the chicken fingers there too.

8. Cook the meal for 12 minutes (6 minutes from each sideat 380 F.

9. When the meal is cooked – let it chill little and serve!

NUTRITION: Calories 334, Fat 22.4, Fiber 2.1, Carbs 4.2, Protein 29.6

14.Egg Salad with Avocado

Preparation time: 12 minutes • Cooking time: 15 minutes • Servings:

6

INGREDIENTS

- 2sweet peppers, chopped

- 1red onion, sliced

- 1avocado, chopped

- 3eggs

- 1tomato, chopped

- 1tablespoon olive oil

- 1teaspoon minced garlic

DIRECTIONS

1. Place the eggs on the air fryer rack and cook them at 250

   F for 15 minutes.

2. After this, place them in the ice water to chill.

3. Then place the chopped sweet peppers in the bowl.

4. Add the sliced onion and chopped avocado.

5. After this, add the minced garlic.

6. Peel the eggs and chop them roughly.

7. Add the eggs to the vegetable bowl.

8. Sprinkle the salad with the olive oil and stir gently.

9. Serve it immediately!

NUTRITION: Calories 142, Fat 11.2, Fiber 3.3, Carbs 8.3, Protein 4.1

15.Juicy Scallops

Preparation time: 15 minutes • Cooking time: 6 minutes • Servings: 2

INGREDIENTS

- 11oz scallops

- 1orange

- ¼ lime

- 1tablespoon olive oil

- ½ teaspoon dried rosemary

- ¼ teaspoon salt

- ¼ teaspoon ground black pepper

DIRECTIONS

1. Grate the orange zest and squeeze the juice.

2. Mix up together the orange juice and orange zest.

3. Stir it carefully and add dried rosemary and salt.

4. Sprinkle the mixture with the ground black pepper.

5. Squeeze the juice from the lime and add it to the

mixture.

6. Whisk it well.

7. Pour the liquid mixture over the scallops and leave them for at least 6 minutes to marinate.

8. After this, pour the olive oil in the air fryer basket and add the marinated scallops.

9. Cook the seafood for 6 minutes at 400 F. Flip the scallops into another side after 3 minutes of cooking.

10. Serve the cooked meal immediately.

NUTRITION: Calories 245, Fat 8.4, Fiber 2.6, Carbs 15.7, Protein 27.1

CHAPTER 3

SIDES

16.Parsnip Fries

Cooking Time: 12 minutes • Servings: 2

INGREDIENTS

- 2tablespoons of olive oil

- A pinch of sea salt 1large bunch of parsnips

DIRECTIONS 1. Wash and peel the parsnips, then cut them into strips. Place the parsnips in a bowl with the olive oil and sea salt and coat well. Preheat your air fryer to 360°Fahrenheit. Place the parsnip and oil mixture into the air fryer basket. Cook for 12-minutes. Serve with sour cream or ketchup.

NUTRITION: Calories: 262g, Total Fat: 11.3g, Carbs: 10.4g, Protein: 7.2g

17.Bell Peppers with Potato Stuffing

Cooking Time: 20 minutes • Servings: 4

INGREDIENTS

- 4green bell peppers, top cut and deseeded

- 4potatoes, boiled, peeled and mashed

- 2onions, finely chopped

- 1teaspoon lemon juice

- 2tablespoons coriander leaves, chopped

- 2green chilies, finely chopped

- Olive oil as needed

- Salt to taste

- ¼ teaspoon Garam Masala

- ½ teaspoon chili powder

- ¼ teaspoon turmeric powder

- 1teaspoon cumin seeds

DIRECTIONS

1. Heat the oil in a pan and sauté the onion, chilies and cumin seeds. Add the rest of the ingredients except

the bell peppers and mix well. Preheat your air fryer to 390°Fahrenheit for 10-minutes. Brush your bell peppers with olive oil, inside and out and stuff each pepper with potato mixture. Place in air fryer basket and grill for 10-minutes. Check and grill for an additional 5-minutes.

NUTRITION: Calories: 282, Total Fat: 9.2g, Carbs: 7.1g, Protein: 4.2g

18.Eggplant Parmesan Panini

Cooking Time: 25 minutes • Servings: 2

INGREDIENTS

- 1medium eggplant, cut into ½ inch slices

- ½ cup mayonnaise

- 2tablespoons milk

- Black pepper to taste

- ½ teaspoon garlic powder

- ½ teaspoon onion powder

- 1tablespoon dried parsley

- ½ teaspoon Italian seasoning

- ½ cup breadcrumbs

- Sea salt to taste

- Fresh basil, chopped for garnishing

- ¾ cup tomato sauce

- 2tablespoons parmesan, grated cheese

- 2cups grated mozzarella cheese

- 2tablespoons olive oil

- 4slices artisan Italian bread

- Cooking spray

DIRECTIONS

1. Cover both sides of eggplant with salt. Place them between sheets of paper towels. Set aside for 30-minutes to get rid of excess moisture. In a mixing bowl, combine Italian seasoning, breadcrumbs, parsley, onion powder, garlic powder and season with salt and pepper. In another small bowl, whisk mayonnaise and milk until smooth.

2. Preheat your air fryer to 400°Fahrenheit. Remove the excess salt from eggplant slices. Cover both sides of eggplant with mayonnaise mixture. Press the eggplant slices into the breadcrumb

   mixture. Use cooking spray on both sides of eggplant slices. Air fry slices in batches for 15-minutes, turning over when halfway done. Each bread slice must be greased with olive oil. On a cutting board, place two slices of bread with oiled sides down. Layer mozzarella cheese and grated parmesan cheese. Place eggplant on cheese. Cover with tomato sauce and add remaining mozzarella and parmesan cheeses. Garnish with chopped fresh basil. Put the second slice of bread oiled side up on top. Take preheated Panini press and place sandwiches on it. Close the lid and cook for 10-minutes. Slice panini into halves and serve.

NUTRITION: Calories: 267, Total Fat: 11.3g, Carbs: 8.7g, Protein: 8.5g

19.Spinach Samosa

Cooking Time: 15 minutes • Servings: 2

INGREDIENTS

- 1½ cups of almond flour

- ½ teaspoon baking soda

- 1teaspoon garam masala

- 1teaspoon coriander, chopped

- ¼ cup green peas

- ½ teaspoon sesame seeds

- ¼ cup potatoes, boiled, small chunks

- 2tablespoons olive oil

- ¾ cup boiled and blended spinach puree

- Salt and chili powder to taste

DIRECTIONS

1. In a bowl, mix baking soda, salt, and flour to make the dough. Add 1-tablespoon of oil. Add the spinach puree and mix until the dough is smooth. Place in fridge for twenty-minutes. In the pan add one

tablespoon of oil, then add potatoes, peas and cook for 5-minutes. Add the sesame seeds, garam masala, coriander, and stir. Knead the dough and make the small ball using a rolling pin. Form balls, make into cone shapes, which are then filled with stuffing that is not yet fully cooked. Make sure flour sheets are well sealed. Preheat air fryer to 390°Fahrenheit. Place samosa in air fryer basket and cook for 10-minutes.

NUTRITION: Calories: 254, Total Fat: 12.2g, Carbs: 9.3g, Protein: 10.2g

20.   Avocado Fries

Cooking Time: 10 minutes • Servings: 4

INGREDIENTS

- 1-ounce aquafina

- 1avocado, sliced

- ½ teaspoon salt

- ½ cup panko breadcrumbs

DIRECTIONS

1. Toss the panko breadcrumbs and salt together in a bowl. Pour Aquafina into another bowl. Dredge the avocado slices in Aquafina and then panko breadcrumbs. Arrange the slices in single layer in air fryer basket. Air fry at 0°Fahrenheit for 10-minutes.

NUTRITION: Calories: 263,   Total   Fat: 7.4g, Carbs: 6.5g, Protein: 8.2g

CHAPTER 4

SEAFOOD

21. Tilapia and Tomato

Preparation Time: 25 minutes Servings:4

INGREDIENTS

- 4tilapia fillets; boneless and halved

- ¼ cup tomato paste

- 1cup tomatoes; cubed

- 1cup roasted peppers; chopped.

- 2tbsp. olive oil

- 1tbsp. lemon juice

- 1tsp. oregano; dried

- 1tsp. garlic powder Salt and black pepper to taste.

DIRECTIONS

1. In a baking dish that fits your air fryer, mix the
   fish with all the other ingredients, toss.

2. Introduce in your air fryer and cook at 380°F for 20 minutes. Divide into bowls and serve

NUTRITION: Calories: 250; Fat: 9g; Fiber: 2g; Carbs: 5g; Protein: 14g

CHAPTER 5

POULTRY

22.   Stuffed Chicken and Baked Potatoes

Preparation time: 10-20Minutes • Cooking time: 45-60 • Servings: 4

INGREDIENTS

- 800 g boneless chicken

- 300 g minced meat

- 150 g sausage

- 80 g French toast

- 1tbsp chopped parsley

DIRECTION:

1. Bone the chicken (or bone directly by the butcher).

2. Prepare the filling:

3. Put in a food processor the meat, the sausage, the French

    toast bathed in milk to soften it, the parsley, the eggs, the grated cheese, the salt, the pepper and mix until obtaining a homogeneous and compact mixture.

4. Fill the boneless chicken and tie it well with a kitchen rope so that the filling does not come out.

5. Place the chicken inside the bowl, add the chopped potatoes, oil, salt, and pepper.

6. Set the air fryer to 1600C. Cook everything for 60 minutes over mix the potatoes 2-3 times to cook evenly and turn the chicken about once in the middle of cooking.

NUTRITION: Calories 223.8 Fat 6.5 g Carbohydrate 19.8 g Sugars 1.9 g Protein21.2 g Cholesterol 48.8 mg

23.   Tandoori Chicken

Preparation time: more than 30Minutes • Cooking time: 15 – 30 •

Servings: 4

INGREDIENTS

- 600 g chicken pieces

- 125 g whole yogurt

- 1tbsp curry

- 3tsp of spices for roasted meats

DIRECTION:

1. Place all ingredients in a bowl, flame well and let stand for 1 hour in the refrigerator.

2. Place the pieces of meat in the basket and set the temperature to 1600C

3. Cook the meat for 30 minutes, turning it 1-2 times to brown the chicken on both sides.

NUTRITION: Calories 263 Fat 12g Carbohydrates 6.1g Sugars 3.7g Protein 31g Cholesterol 135mg

24.   Crispy Chicken Fillets in Brine in Pickle Juice

Preparation time: 10 minutes • Cooking time: 12 minutes • Servings: 4

INGREDIENTS

- 12chicken offers (1 ¼ pounds in total
- 1¼ cups pickled dill juice
- 1large egg
- 1large egg white
- ½ tsp kosher salt
- Freshly ground black pepper
- ½ cup seasoned breadcrumbs, regular or gluten free
- ½ cup seasoned breadcrumbs, regular or gluten free
- Olive oil spray

DIRECTION:

1. Place the chicken in a shallow bowl and cover with the pickle juice (enough to cover completely). Cover and marine for 8 hours in the refrigerator.

2. Drain the chicken and dry it completely with a paper towel (discard the marinade). In a medium bowl, beat the whole egg, egg white, salt, and pepper. In a shallow arch, combine the breadcrumbs.

3. Dip the chicken in the egg mixture, piece by piece, then in the breadcrumbs, pressing lightly. Remove excess breadcrumbs and place it on a work surface. Spray generously both sides of the chicken with oil.

4. Preheat the fryer to 400°F.

5. Working in batches, place a single layer of chicken in the fryer basket. Cook 10 to 12 minutes, turning halfway through cooking, until cooked, crispy and golden brown. (For a toaster-style air fryer, the temperature stays the same; cook for about 10 minutes.

NUTRITION: Calories: 244kcal Carbohydrates 10g Protein: 37g Fat: 6g Cholesterol 150mg Sugar 1g

25. Chicken, Leeks and Coriander Mix

Preparation time: 10 minutes • Cooking time: 20 minutes •

Servings: 4

INGREDIENTS

- 2pounds chicken breast, skinless, boneless and halved

- 2leeks, sliced

- 2tablespoons coriander, chopped

- 1tablespoon turmeric powder

- 1tablespoon sweet paprika

- Salt and black pepper to the taste

- 2tablespoons olive oil

- 1tablespoon chives, chopped

DIRECTIONS

1. In the air fryer's pan, mix the chicken with the leeks and the other ingredients, cook at 370 degrees F for 20 minutes, divide between plates and serve.

NUTRITION: Calories 270, Fat 11, Fiber 11, Carbs 17, Protein 11

CHAPTER 6

MEAT

26.   Homemade Flamingos

Preparation time: 10 minutes • Cooking time: 20 minutes • Servings:

6

INGREDIENTS

- 6pieces of Serrano ham, thinly sliced

- 454g pork, halved, with butter and crushed

- 6g of salt 1g black pepper

- 227g fresh spinach leaves, divided

- 4slices of mozzarella cheese, divided

- 18g sun-dried tomatoes, divided

- 10ml of olive oil, divided

DIRECTION:

1. Place 3 pieces of ham on baking paper, slightly overlapping

each other. Place 1 half of the pork in the ham. Repeat with the other half.

2. Season the inside of the pork rolls with salt and pepper.

3. Place half of the spinach, cheese, and sun-dried tomatoes on top of the pork loin, leaving a 13 mm border on all sides.

4. Roll the fillet around the filling well and tie with a kitchen cord to keep it closed.

5. Repeat the process for the other pork steak and place them in the fridge.

6. Select Preheat in the air fryer and press Start/Pause.

7. Brush 5 ml of olive oil on each wrapped steak and place them in the preheated air fryer.

8. Select Steak. Set the timer to 9 minutes and press Start/Pause.

9. Allow it to cool for 10 minutes before cutting.

NUTRITION: Calories: 424 Fat: 15.15g Carbohydrates: 37.47g Protein: 31.84g Sugar: 3.37g Cholesterol: 157mg

27.   North Carolina Style Pork Chops

Preparation time: 5 minutes • Cooking time: 10 minutes •
Servings: 2

INGREDIENTS

- 2boneless pork chops
- 15ml of vegetable oil
- 25g dark brown sugar, packaged
- 6g of Hungarian paprika
- 2g ground mustard
- 2g freshly ground black pepper
- 3g onion powder
- 3g garlic powder
- Salt and pepper to taste

DIRECTION:

1. Preheat the air fryer a few minutes at 1800C.

2. Cover the pork chops with oil.

3. Put all the spices and season the pork chops abundantly, almost as if you were making them breaded.

4. Place the pork chops in the preheated air fryer.

5. Select Steak, set the time to 10 minutes.

6. Remove the pork chops when it has finished cooking. Let it stand for 5 minutes and serve.

NUTRITION: Calories: 118 Fat: 6.85g Carbohydrates: 0 Protein: 13.12g Sugar: 0g Cholesterol: 39mg

28.   Stuffed Cabbage and Pork Loin Rolls

Preparation time: 5 minutes • Cooking time: 25 minutes Servings: 4

INGREDIENTS

- 500g of white cabbage

- 1onion

- 8pork tenderloin steaks

- 2carrots

- 4tbsp soy sauce

- 50g of olive oil

- Salt

- 8sheets of rice

DIRECTION:

1. Put the chopped cabbage in the Thermomix glass together with the onion and the chopped carrot.

2. Select 5 seconds, speed Add the extra virgin olive oil. Select 5 minutes, varoma temperature, left turn, spoon speed.

3. Cut the tenderloin steaks into thin strips. Add the meat

to the Thermomix glass. Select 5 minutes, varoma temperature, left turn, spoon speed. Without beaker

4. Add the soy sauce. Select 5 minutes, varoma temperature, left turn, spoon speed. Rectify salt. Let it cold down.

5. Hydrate the rice slices. Extend and distribute the filling between them.

6. Make the rolls, folding so that the edges are completely closed. Place the rolls in the air fryer and paint with the oil.

7. Select 10 minutes, 1800C.

NUTRITION: Calories: 120 Fat: 3.41g Carbohydrates: 0g Protein: 20.99g Sugar: 0g Cholesterol: 65mg

CHAPTER 7

VEGETABLES

29.   Green salad with roasted pepper

Preparation time: 5 minutes • Cooking time: 10 minutes • Servings: 2

INGREDIENTS

- 1red pepper

- 1tbsp lemon juice

- 3tbsp yogurt

- 2tbsp olive oil

- Freshly ground black pepper

- 1romaine lettuce, cut into large strips

- 50g arugula leaves

DIRECTION:

1. Preheat the Air Fryer to 200°C.

2. Place the pepper in the basket and insert it into the Air

Fryer. Set the timer for 10 minutes and roast the pepper until the skin is slightly burned.

3. Then cut the pepper into quarters and remove the seeds and skin. Cut the pepper into strips.

4. Prepare vinaigrette in a bowl with 2 tablespoons of pepper juice, lemon juice, yogurt, and olive oil. Add pepper and salt according to your taste.

5. Mix the lettuce and arugula leaves in the vinaigrette and garnish the salad with the pepper strips.

NUTRITION: Calories 47.3 Fat 0.4 g Carbohydrate 10.8 g Sugars 2.0 g Protein1.8 g Cholesterol 0.0 mg

30. Pumpkin Spice Pecans

Preparation Time: 11 minutes • Servings: 4

INGREDIENTS

- 1cup whole pecans

- 1large egg. white

- ¼ cup granular erythritol.

- ½ tsp. pumpkin pie spice

- ½ tsp. vanilla extract.

- ½ tsp. ground cinnamon.

DIRECTIONS

1. Toss all ingredients in a large bowl until pecans are coated. Place into the air fryer basket.

2. Adjust the temperature to 300 Degrees F and set the timer for 6 minutes. Toss two to three times during cooking. Allow to cool completely. Store in an airtight container up to 3 days

NUTRITION: Calories: 178; Protein: 3.2g; Fiber: 2.6g; Fat: 17.0g; Carbs: 19.0g

31. Cream Puffs

Preparation Time: 21 minutes Servings: 8

puffs

INGREDIENTS

- 2oz. full-fat cream cheese.

- 1large egg. ¼ cup powdered erythritol

- ½ cup blanched finely ground almond flour.

- ½ cup low-carb vanilla protein powder

- ½ cup granular erythritol.

- 2tbsp. heavy whipping cream.

- 5tbsp. unsalted butter; melted.

- ½ tsp. baking powder. ¼ tsp. ground cinnamon.

- ½ tsp. vanilla extract.

DIRECTIONS

1. Mix almond flour, protein powder, granular erythritol, baking powder, egg and butter in a large bowl until a soft dough forms.

2. Place the dough in the freezer for 20 minutes. Wet

your hands with water and roll the dough into eight balls.

3. Cut a piece of parchment to fit your air fryer basket. Working in batches as necessary, place the dough balls into the air fryer basket on top of parchment.

4. Adjust the temperature to 380 Degrees F and set the timer for 6 minutes. Flip cream puffs halfway through the cooking time.

5. When the timer beeps, remove the puffs and allow to cool.

6. Take a medium bowl, beat the cream cheese, powdered erythritol, cinnamon, cream and vanilla until fluffy.

7. Place the mixture into a pastry bag or a storage bag with the end snipped. Cut a small hole in the bottom of each puff and fill with some of the cream mixture. Store in an airtight container up to 2 days in the refrigerator.

NUTRITION: Calories: 178; Protein: 14.9g; Fiber: 1.3g; Fat: 12.1g; Carbs: 22.1g

32.   Chard and Olives

Preparation time: 5 minutes • Cooking time: 20 minutes •
Servings: 4

INGREDIENTS

- 2cups red chard, torn

- 1cup kalamata olives, pitted and halved

- ½ cup tomato sauce

- 1teaspoon chili powder

- 2tablespoons olive oil

- Salt and black pepper to the taste

DIRECTIONS

1. In a pan that fits the air fryer, combine the chard with
   the olives and the other ingredients and toss.

2. Put the pan in your air fryer, cook at 370 degrees F for
   20 minutes, divide between plates and serve.

NUTRITION: Calories 154, Fat 3, Fiber 2, Carbs 4, Protein 6

CHAPTER 8

SNACKS

33.   Avocado Bites

Preparation Time: 13 minutes Servings: 4

INGREDIENTS

- 4avocados, peeled, pitted and cut into wedges

- 1½ cups almond meal

- 1egg; whisked

- A pinch of salt and black pepper

- Cooking spray

DIRECTIONS

1. Put the egg in a bowl and the almond meal in another.

2. Season avocado wedges with salt and pepper, coat them in egg and then in meal almond

3. Arrange the avocado bites in your air fryer's basket,

grease them with cooking spray and cook at 400°F for 8

minutes Servings as a snack right away

NUTRITION: Calories: 200; Fat: 12g; Fiber: 3g; Carbs: 5g;

Protein: 16g

34.   Cayenne Almonds

Preparation time: 5 minutes • Cooking time: 10 minutes • Servings: 6

INGREDIENTS

- 1egg white

- 3cups whole almonds

- 2tsp salt

- 2tsp cayenne pepper

- ½ tsp ground black pepper

DIRECTIONS:

1. Preheat your air fryer to 325 degrees F and prepare the air fryer tray with parchment paper.

2. Place the egg whites in a large bowl and whip until stiff peaks form.

3. Add the almonds and toss to coat.

4. Sprinkle with the seasonings and then place the almonds on the tray, laying them out as evenly as possible on the tray.

5. Bake in the air fryer for 10 minutes. The almonds

should be golden brown.

6. Remove from the air fryer and let cool.

NUTRITION: Calories 414, Total Fat 34g, Saturated Fat 8g, Total Carbs 14g, Net Carbs 7g, Protein 14, Sugar 2g, Fiber 8g, Sodium 210mg, Potassium 0g

35.   **Black Pepper Almonds**

Preparation time: 5 minutes • Cooking time: 10 minutes • Servings: 6

INGREDIENTS

- 1egg white 3cups whole almonds

- 2tsp salt 1tsp ground black pepper

DIRECTIONS:

1. Preheat your air fryer to 325 degrees F and prepare the air fryer tray with parchment paper.

2. Place the egg whites in a large bowl and whip until stiff peaks form.

3. Add the almonds and toss to coat.

4. Sprinkle with the salt and pepper and then place the almonds on the tray, laying them out as evenly as possible on the tray.

5. Bake in the air fryer for 10 minutes. The almonds should be golden brown.Remove from the air fryer and let cool.

NUTRITION: Calories 414, Total Fat 34g, Saturated Fat 8g, Total Carbs 14g, Net Carbs 7g, Protein 14, Sugar 2g, Fiber 8g, Sodium 210mg, Potassium 0g

36. Air-Fried Sesame Tofu with Broccoli & Bell Pepper Salad

Cooking Time: 20 minutes • Servings: 5

INGREDIENTS

- ¾ cups red bell pepper, sliced

- 1cup broccoli

- 1teaspoon sesame oil

- 1teaspoon olive oil

- 1tablespoon lemon zest

- 1tablespoon Shaoxing wine

- Salt and pepper to taste

- 1tablespoon sriracha sauce

- 1tablespoon sugar-free syrup

- ½ cup sesame seeds

- 1cup of tofu

DIRECTIONS

1. Prepare broccoli and red bell pepper. Soak the broccoli in warm water and rinse in cold water. Cut it

into florets and set aside. Slice the red pepper into cubes. In a bowl, mix vegetables. Add Shaoxing wine, olive oil, lemon zest into bowl, season with salt and pepper and toss to combine. Rinse and drain a cup of tofu. Cut tofu into small cubes. Place tofu in mixing bowl, add sesame seeds to the bowl. Season with sriracha sauce and syrup. Mix well. Preheat your air-fryer to 370°Fahrenheit for 2-minutes. Place tofu mixture into air-fryer and spray it with sesame oil. Cook the tofu mixture for 20- minutes. Shake the basket a few times through cook time. Add the tofu to the bowl of veggies and toss. Serve right away

NUTRITION: Calories: 340, Total Fat: 18g, Carbs: 18g, Protein: 22g

37.　Coconut Pumpkin Curry

Cooking Time: 25 minutes • Servings: 4

INGREDIENTS

- 2cups pumpkin, cubed

- 1tablespoon sesame seeds

- 2-inches ginger, minced

- 1tablespoon parsley, chopped

- 2teaspoons curry powder

- 1teaspoon black pepper

- ¼ cup coconut cream

- 1tablespoon shredded coconut

- 1red chili for garnish

- 1red chili, minced

- ¼ cup water

DIRECTIONS

1. Place the cubed pumpkin into the pan with minced ginger.

Add ¼ cup water and ¼ cup coconut cream into the pan.

Cook for 　　15-minutes at 300°Fahrenheit. Slightly

mash pumpkin cubes. Add the minced chili, curry powder, pepper, and stir. Cook for another 10-minutes. Transfer to a large bowl. Garnish with chopped parsley and red chili. Serve warm.

NUTRITION: Calories: 115, Total Fat: 4.38g, Carbs: 19.85, Protein: 2.7g

CHAPTER 9

DESSERT

38.   Olives and Cilantro Vinaigrette

Preparation Time: 17 minutes • Servings: 4

INGREDIENTS

- 1cup baby spinach

- 2cups black olives, pitted

- 1tbsp. olive oil

- 2tbsp. balsamic vinegar

- A bunch of cilantro; chopped.

- Salt and black pepper to taste.

DIRECTIONS

1. In a pan that fits the air fryer, combine all the ingredients and toss.

2. Put the pan in the air fryer and cook at 370°F for 12

minutes

3. Transfer to bowls and serve.

NUTRITION: Calories: 132; Fat: 4g; Fiber: 2g; Carbs: 4g;

Protein: 4g

39. Broccoli and Tomatoes

Preparation Time: 20 minutes • Servings: 4

INGREDIENTS

- 1broccoli head, florets separated

- 2cups cherry tomatoes, quartered

- 1tbsp. cilantro; chopped.

- Juice of 1 lime

- A drizzle of olive oil

- A pinch of salt and black pepper

DIRECTIONS

1. In a pan that fits the air fryer, combine the broccoli with tomatoes and the rest of the ingredients except the cilantro, toss, put the pan in the air fryer and cook at 380°F for 15 minutes

2. Divide between plates and serve with cilantro sprinkled on top.

NUTRITION: Calories: 141; Fat: 3g; Fiber: 2g; Carbs: 4g; Protein: 5g

40. Kale and Mushrooms

Preparation Time: 20 minutes • Servings: 4

INGREDIENTS

- 1lb. brown mushrooms; sliced

- 1lb. kale, torn

- 14oz. coconut milk

- 2tbsp. olive oil

- Salt and black pepper to taste.

DIRECTIONS

1. In a pan that fits your air fryer, mix the kale with the rest of the ingredients and toss

2. Put the pan in the fryer, cook at 380°F for 15 minutes, divide between plates and serve

NUTRITION: Calories: 162; Fat: 4g; Fiber: 1g; Carbs: 3g; Protein: 5g

41. Spicy Olives and Avocado

Preparation Time: 20 minutes • Servings: 4

INGREDIENTS

- 2small avocados, pitted; peeled and sliced

- ¼ cup cherry tomatoes; halved

- 2cups kalamata olives, pitted

- 1tbsp. coconut oil; melted

- juice of 1 lime

DIRECTIONS:

1. In a pan that fits the air fryer, combine the olives with the other ingredients, toss.

2. Put the pan in your air fryer and cook at 370°F for 15 minutes

3. Divide the mix between plates and serve.

NUTRITION: Calories: 153; Fat: 3g; Fiber: 3g; Carbs: 4g; Protein: 6g

42.   Lemon Endives

Preparation Time: 20 minutes • Servings: 4

INGREDIENTS

- 12endives, trimmed

- 3tbsp. ghee; melted

- 1tbsp. lemon juice

- A pinch of salt and black pepper

DIRECTIONS

1. take a bowl and mix the endives with the ghee, salt, pepper and lemon juice and toss.

2. put the endives in the fryer's basket and cook at 350°f for 15 minutes

3. divide between plates and serve.

NUTRITION: Calories: 163; Fat: 4g; Fiber: 3g; Carbs: 5g; Protein: 6g

43.   Blueberry Cream

Preparation Time: 24 minutes • Servings: 6

INGREDIENTS

- 2cups blueberries

- 2tbsp. swerve

- 2tbsp. water

- 1tsp. vanilla extract

- Juice of ½ lemon

DIRECTIONS

1. Take a bowl and mix all the ingredients and whisk well.

2. Divide this into 6 ramekins, put them in the air fryer and

   cook at 340°F for 20 minutes.

3. Cool down and serve

NUTRITION: Calories: 123; Fat: 2g; Fiber: 2g; Carbs: 4g; Protein: 3g

44.   Strawberry Jam

Preparation Time: 30 minutes • Servings: 12

INGREDIENTS

- 8oz. strawberries; sliced
- ¼ cup swerve
- ¼ cup water
- 1tbsp. lemon juice

DIRECTIONS

1. In a pan that fits the air fryer, combine all the ingredients.

2. Put the pan in the machine and cook at 380°F for 20 minutes

3. Divide the mix into cups, cool down and serve.

NUTRITION: Calories: 100; Fat: 1g; Fiber: 0g; Carbs: 1g; Protein: 1g

45. Lemon Cookies

Preparation Time: 30 minutes • Servings: 12

INGREDIENTS

- ¼ cup cashew butter, soft

- 1egg, whisked

- ¾ cup swerve

- 1cup coconut cream

- Juice of 1 lemon

- 1tsp. baking powder

- 1tsp. lemon peel, grated

DIRECTIONS

1. In a bowl, combine all the ingredients gradually and stir well.

2. Spoon balls this on a cookie sheet lined with parchment paper and flatten them.

3. Put the cookie sheet in the fryer and cook at 350°F for 20 minutesServings the cookies cold

NUTRITION: Calories: 121; Fat: 5g; Fiber: 1g; Carbs: 4g; Protein: 2g

46.   Vanilla Spiced Soufflé

Preparation Time: 20 minutes • Cooking Time: 32 minutes •

Servings: 6

INGREDIENTS

- ¼ cup all-purpose flour

- 1cup whole milk

- 2tsps. vanilla extract

- 1tsp. cream of tartar

- 1vanilla bean

- 4egg yolks

- 1-oz. Sugar ¼ cup softened butter

- ¼ cup sugar 5egg whites

DIRECTIONS

1. Combine flour and butter in a bowl until the mixture becomes a smooth paste.

2. Set the pan over medium flame to heat the milk. Add sugar and stir until dissolved.

3. Mix in the vanilla bean and bring to a boil.

4. Beat the mixture using a wire whisk as you add the butter and flour mixture.

5. Lower the heat to simmer until thick. Discard the vanilla bean. Turn off the heat.

6. Place them on an ice bath and allow to cool for 10 minutes.

7. Grease 6 ramekins with butter. Sprinkle each with a bit of sugar.

8. Beat the egg yolks in a bowl. Add the vanilla extract and milk mixture. Mix until combined.

9. Whisk together the tartar cream, egg whites, and sugar until it forms medium stiff peaks.

10. Gradually fold egg whites into the soufflé base. Transfer the mixture to the ramekins.

11. Put 3 ramekins in the cooking basket at a time. Cook for 16 minutes at 330 degrees. Move to a wire rack for cooling and cook the rest.

12. Sprinkle powdered sugar on top and drizzle with chocolate sauce before serving.

NUTRITION: Calories: 215 Fat: 12.2g   Carbs: 18.98g Protein: 6.66g

47.   Apricot Blackberry Crumble

Preparation Time: 10 minutes • Cooking Time: 20 minutes •

Servings: 8

INGREDIENTS

- 1cup flour

- 18oz. fresh apricots

- 5tbsps. cold butter

- ½ cup sugar

- 5½ oz. fresh blackberries

- Salt

- 2tbsps. lemon juice

DIRECTIONS

1. Put the apricots and blackberries in a bowl. Add lemon

   juice and 2 tbsps. of sugar. Mix until combined.

2. Transfer the mixture to a baking dish.

3. Put flour, the rest of the sugar, and a pinch of salt in a

   bowl. Mix well. Add a tbsp. of cold butter.

4. Combine the mixture until it becomes crumbly. Put

this on top of the fruit mixture and press it down lightly.

5. Set the baking tray in the cooking basket.

6. Cook for 20 minutes at 390 degrees.

7. Allow to cool before slicing and serving.

NUTRITION: Calories: 217Fat: 7.44g   Carbs: 36.2g

Protein: 2.3g

48. Chocolate Cup cakes

Preparation Time: 5 minutes • Cooking Time: 12 minutes •

Servings: 6

INGREDIENTS

- 3eggs

- ¼ cup caster sugar

- ¼ cup cocoa powder

- 1tsp. baking powder

- 1cup milk

- ¼ tsp. vanilla essence

- 2cup all-purpose flour

- 4tbsps. butter

DIRECTIONS

1. Preheat your Air Fryer to a temperature of 400°F (200°C).

2. Beat eggs with sugar in a bowl until creamy.

3. Add butter and beat again for 1-2 minutes.

4. Now add flour, cocoa powder, milk, baking powder, and

vanilla essence, mix with a spatula.

5. Fill ¾ of muffin tins with the mixture and place them into Air Fryer basket.

6. Let cook for 12 minutes.

7. Serve!

NUTRITION: Calories: 289 Protein: 8.72 g Fat: 11.5 g Carbs: 38.94 g

49.   Stuffed Baked Apples

Preparation Time: 3 minutes • Cooking Time: 12 minutes •
Servings: 4

INGREDIENTS

- 4tbsps. Honey ¼ cup brown sugar

- ½ cup raisins ½ cup crushed walnuts

- 4large apples

DIRECTIONS:

1. Preheat Air Fryer to a temperature of 350°F (180°C).

2. Cut the apples from the stem and remove the inner using spoon.

3. Now fill each apple with raisins, walnuts, honey, and brown sugar.

4. Transfer apples in a pan and place in Air Fryer basket, cook for 12 minutes.

5. Serve.

NUTRITION: Calories: 324 Protein: 2.8 g Fat: 6.99 g Carbs: 70.31 g

50.   Roasted Pineapples with Vanilla Zest

Preparation Time: 5 minutes • Cooking Time: 8 minutes •

Servings: 4

INGREDIENTS

- 2anise stars

- ¼ cup orange juice

- 1tsp. lime juice

- 1vanilla pod

- 2tbsps. caster sugar

- ¼ cup pineapple juice

- 1lb. pineapple slices

DIRECTIONS

1. Preheat Air Fryer to a temperature of 350°F (180°C).

2. Take a baking pan that can fit into Air Fryer basket.

3. Now add pineapple juice, sugar, orange juice, anise stars, and vanilla pod into a pan and mix well.

4. Place in pineapple slices evenly and transfer pan into Air Fryer basket.

5. Cook for 8 minutes.

6. Serve!

NUTRITION: Calories: 90   Protein: 0.79 g Fat: 1.17 g Carbs:

23.22 g

51.Apricots Cream

Preparation time: 10 minutes • Cooking time: 15 minutes • Servings: 4

INGREDIENTS

- 1cup apricots, chopped

- 1cup heavy cream

- 2tablespoons sugar

- 1teaspoon ginger, grated

DIRECTIONS

1. In the air fryer's pan, mix the apricots with the cream and the other ingredients, whisk, introduce the pan in the air fryer and cook at 380 degrees F for 15 minutes.

2. Divide into bowls and serve.

NUTRITION: Calories 200, Fat 3, Fiber 4, Carbs 11, Protein 3

52.   **Ginger Cake**

Preparation time: 10 minutes • Cooking time: 30 minutes •
Servings: 4

INGREDIENTS

- 1cup almond flour

- 2tablespoons ginger, grated

- 1cup heavy cream

- 1teaspoon baking powder

- 3tablespoons sugar

- ½ cup coconut cream

- 1teaspoon cinnamon powder

- 3tablespoons butter, melted

- 4eggs, whisked

DIRECTIONS

1. In a bowl, mix the flour with the ginger, cream and the
   other ingredients, stir well, pour this into a lined cake
   pan, introduce the pan in the fryer and cook at 370
   degrees F for 30 minutes.

2. Leave the cake to cool down, slice and serve.

NUTRITION: Calories 213, Fat 3, Fiber 6, Carbs 15, Protein 4

DAY MEAL PLAN

DAY	BREAKFAST	MAINS	DESSERTS
1.	Stuffed Portobello Mushrooms with Ground Beef	Indian Chickpeas	Butter Cookies
2.	Basil-Spinach Quiche	White Beans with Rosemary	Cream Cheese and Zucchinis Bars
3.	Stuffed Chicken Roll with Mushrooms	Squash Bowls	Coconut Cookies
4.	Eggs on Avocado Burgers	Cauliflower tew with Tomatoes and Green Chilies	Lemon Cookies
5.	Applesauce Mash with Sweet Potato	Simple Quinoa Stew	Delicious cheesecake
6.	Bacon and Kale Breakfast Salad	Green Beans with Carrot	Macaroons
7.	Fish Fritatta	Chickpeas and Lentils Mix	Amaretto and bread dough
8.	Spinach Frittata	Garlic Pork Chops	Orange cake
9.	Kale Quiche with Eggs	Honey Ginger Salmon	Apple bread

		Steaks	
10.	Olives Rice Mix	Mustard Pork Balls	Strawberry pie
11.	Sweet Quinoa Mix	Beef Meatballs in Tomato Sauce	Bread pudding
12.	Creamy Almond Rice	Green Stuffed Peppers	Pomegranate and chocolate bars
13.	Chives Quinoa Bowls	Sweet & Sour Chicken Skewer	Crisp apples
14.	Potato Casserole	Lamb Meatballs	Cocoa cookies
15.	Turkey and Peppers Bowls	Spiced Green Beans with Veggies	Strawberry shortcakes
16.	Turkey Tortillas	Chipotle Green Beans	Lentils and dates brownies
17.	Avocado Eggs Mix	Tomato and Cranberry Beans Pasta	Chocolate cookies
18.	Maple Apple Quinoa	Mexican Casserole	Mini lava cakes
19.	Chopped Kale with Ground Beef	Spicy Herb Chicken Wings	Banana bread
20.	Bacon Wrapped Chicken Fillet	Roasted Cauliflower with Nuts & Raisins	Granola
21.	Egg Whites with Sliced Tomatoes	Red Potatoes with Green	Tomato cake

		Beans and Chutney	
22.	Beef Balls with Sesame and Dill	Simple Italian Veggie Salad	Chocolate cake
23.	Zucchini Rounds with Ground Chicken	Spiced Brown Rice with Mung Beans	Coffee cheesecakes
24.	Meatball Breakfast Salad	Eggplant and Tomato Sauce	Fried banana
25.	Tomatoes with Chicken	Lemony Endive Mix	Banana cake
26.	Cherry Tomatoes Fritatta	Lentils and Spinach Casserole	Espresso cream and pears
27.	Whisked Eggs with Ground Chicken	Scallions and Endives with Rice	Lime cheesecakes Wrapped Pears
28.	Breakfast Bacon Hash	Cabbage and Tomatoes	Strawberry cobbler
29.	Eggplant and weet Potato Hash	Lemon Halibut	Almond and cocoa bars
30.	Eggs in Avocado	Medium-Rare Beef Steak	Ginger cheesecake
31.	Spaghetti Squash Casserole Cups	Fried Cod & Spring Onion	Plum cake